Alessio Brandolini

MINIATURE CITIES

Translated by
Giorgio Mobili

Fomite
Burlington, VT

ISBN-13: 978-978-1-959984-09-2
Library of Congress Control Number: 2023934360
Fomite
58 Peru Street
Burlington, VT 05401
04/06/2023

MINIATURE CITIES

Le città come i sogni sono costruite di desideri e di paure, anche se il filo del loro discorso è segreto, le loro regole assurde, le prospettive ingannevoli, e ogni cosa ne nasconde un'altra.

Cities, like dreams, are made of desires and fears, even if the thread of their discourse is secret, their rules absurd, their perspectives deceptive, and everything conceals something else.

ITALO CALVINO, *Invisible Cities*

Contents

1

POEMS OF THE EARTH

(Poesie della terra, 2004)

to my father

È COME se fossi arrivato
troppo tardi, mi dico
mentre falcio l'erba alta
o annaffio gli ulivi
che hanno appena un anno
piantati con mio padre
dopo aver strappato alla terra
quelli morti, o ammalati.

È come se fossi inchiodato
allo stesso divisorio orientale
o al grattacielo americano
che si disintegra con un boato.
Solido e impenetrabile
calcificato dalla storia
però ugualmente
cito a memoria
i passi lunghi
i più importanti
di questa insolita
ma ben salda deriva.
La promessa è lo stupore
di un solco
preciso e profondo
tracciato non nella polvere
ma nella realtà, nel presente
di questo paterno terreno.

> Come se a sorpresa
> fosse arrivata
> l'ora della semina.

It's AS IF I had arrived
too late, I say to myself
as I mow the tall grass
or water the olive trees
only a year old
which I planted with my father
after we tore out
the ones that were dead or diseased.

It's as if I were nailed
to the very same eastern partition
or to the American skyscraper
disintegrating with a boom.
Solid and impenetrable
calcified by history
yet nonetheless
I quote from memory
the long
and most important passages
from this unusual
though very steadfast drift.
The promise is the wonder
of a furrow
precise and deep
traced not in the dust
but in reality, in the present
of this fatherly ground.

> As if the planting season
> had arrived
> unexpectedly.

Hai un volto
dolce e tranquillo
forse per questo
a volte penso
di conoscerti
da sempre
di poter dialogare
con te, stando seduto
la schiena contro il legno
spianato del castagno
a ripararmi
dai rumori e dal sole.

Qui c'era un pozzo
decenni fa
al centro del terreno
su camion rossi
caricavamo l'uva.

Hai questo volto
dolce e tranquillo
che si ricostruisce da solo
quando provo a raschiarlo
dalle pareti
arcaiche della mente.

You have a sweet
tranquil face
this is perhaps why
I sometimes think
that I've known you
forever
that I can converse
with you as I sit
with my back against the smoothed-down
chestnut's wood
to shield myself
from the noise and the sun.

Decades ago
there was a well here
right in the middle of this plot
we loaded grapes
onto red trucks.

You have this sweet
tranquil face
that reconstructs itself
whenever I attempt to scrape it
off the archaic
walls of my mind.

CERTO NON dissento, e dopo che farei?
Però nel frattempo rinnovo casa
mi trasferisco
in un angolo di strada.
Sì, trasloco fuori città
magari in un bosco
mi stabilisco in una quercia cava.

Un mondo rinforzato da vitamine e sali minerali
certo più sicuro per via degli antifurti
delle porte blindate, dei cancelli sbarrati
con paletti e lucchetto
di libertà sigillate in cassaforte
in attesa di tempi migliori
di un nuovo perfetto equilibrio.

Non sentirò il bisogno
di avere una parte di tutto.
Avrò poco e quel poco mi basterà,
non sentirò la fretta di consumarlo.
Farò a meno di appigli e stampelle
lascerò la porta spalancata
sarò felice di ricevere ospiti e amici.

Tanto la pioggia cancellerà le impronte
diverrà impossibile tornare indietro.

OF COURSE I won't dissent, because then
what would I do?
But meanwhile I renovate
I relocate to a street corner.
Yes, I move out of the city
perhaps into the woods
I take residence in a hollowed oak.

A world reinforced by vitamins and mineral salts
certainly safer thanks to burglar alarms
armored doors, gates secured
with bars and padlocks
liberties sealed in safes
waiting for better times
for a new, perfect equilibrium.

I won't feel the need
to own a part of everything.
I will have little and that little will suffice,
I won't feel the rush to consume it.
I will do without handholds or crutches
I will leave the door wide open
happy to welcome guests and friends.

Besides, the rain will erase all tracks
making it impossible to go back.

I FICHI hanno le dita larghe
le loro foglie sorreggono l'aria
calda di giugno
e le vene scoppiano di gioia.
Anche a settembre danno il frutto
e ce ne sono di quelli neri
ma dolcissimi che strappano
la voglia di fuggire.
Più in là si agitano le foglie
verde-smeraldo del grande susino
giocano con l'aria e per ore
parlano senza un attimo di tregua.

Con la zappa fino al tramonto
ad accarezzare la terra
intorno al tronco
a divorarla con gli occhi.

THE FIG TREES are broad-fingered
their leaves sustain the warm
June air
and the veins burst with joy.
Even in September they yield their fruits
and some are black
yet so sweet that they take away
the longing to flee.
Further away there rustle
the emerald-green leaves of the big plum tree
they play with the air and talk
for hours without a moment's respite.

Until sunset with the hoe
I caress the earth
around the trunk
devouring it with my eyes.

La MUSICA del giardino
oggi scolora
per via di questo sole
impiccato tra i rami
del nespolo e dei noci.
Il prato, poi,
è un logoro cappotto
militare
che certo non protegge
dalle spine
dal timore invernale.

Nuvole basse
hanno perso la strada
l'originaria morbidezza.
Fili di rame
intrecciati nell'aria
riscaldano le foglie
bucano l'erba
i grossi petali
dei curvi girasoli
sfaldano il legno
nodoso degli ulivi.

Ma se qui scavi
trovi schegge di vetro
abbaglianti frammenti
di mosaici romani.

THE MUSIC of the garden
has bleached today
because of this sun
strangled among the branches
of the medlar and the walnut trees.
The lawn, also,
is a threadbare army
coat
certainly no protection
against the thorns
or fear of winter.

Low clouds
have lost their way
their original softness.
Copper threads
interwoven in the air
heat up the leaves
puncture the grass
the huge petals
of the bowing sunflowers
wear away the knotty trunk
of the olive trees.

But if you were to dig here
you'd find glass shards
dazzling fragments
of Roman mosaics.

Più FORTE di un mal di testa
in sostanza privo
di finestre e fondamenta.
Tetti rossi
impiccati tra le nuvole
una gatta miagola
sul filo teso dell'orizzonte.

Non mani né bandiere
salutano il passaggio
vittorioso della notte.

Strade di sabbia
difficile dire se di deserto
che avanza o per il lento
sbriciolamento degli edifici
(guerre o che altro?).

Laggiù, sotto il paese
le querce selvatiche
la terra appena arata.

STRONGER than a headache
in substance devoid
of windows and foundations.
Red roofs
strangled among the clouds
a cat meows
on the taut line of the horizon.

Neither hands nor flags
salute the night's
victorious passage.

Streets of sand
hard to say whether from the encroaching
desert or the slow
crumbling of the buildings
(wars or what else?).

Down there, under the village
the wild oaks
the freshly plowed field.

Il RAMO storto e lungo
per sbaglio non potato
o per trascuratezza
è il solo che resiste.

Col gomito scomposto
affronta le gelate
le malattie dell'aria
anche se sotto
sono arse le zolle di terra
e sanno di caffè
amarissimo
bevuto troppo in fretta.

Il ramo goffo e sghembo
offre sempre il suo frutto.
Pere o ciliegie
una pesca arancione
con due macchie di rosso.

THE TWISTED long branch
left unpruned by mistake
or neglect
is the only one that resists.

With its ungainly elbow
it confronts the frost
the diseases of the air
even though beneath it
the clumps of earth are parched
and taste like coffee
terribly bitter
and too hastily drunk.

The awkward, crooked branch
always offers its fruit.
Pears or cherries
an orange peach
with two red spots.

GLI ALBERI
sono stati abbandonati?
non hanno più nome
sotto la spessa corteccia
c'è solo un buco
un passaggio sbarrato
privo di linfa
un nido di muffa, di tarli.

Per questo fra tre giorni
verranno ad abbatterli.
A terra i frutti
svuotati dai vermi
presi d'assalto
da formiche affamate
dai ragni rossi
con la bocca a tenaglia.

Intorno all'albero
il tappeto di foglie
macerate nell'acqua.

Have the trees
been abandoned?
they no longer have a name
under their thick bark
is but a hole
a blocked conduit
without sap
a nest of mildew, of woodworms.

This is why in three days
they're coming to cut them down.
On the ground, the fruits
hollowed out by worms
stormed
by ravenous ants
by pincer-mouthed
red spiders.

Around the tree
a carpet of leaves
macerated in water.

Limitarsi a poco, sussurri
e io subito aggiungo: virgole
sì, magari ogni tanto
qualche bel punto.

Scavare
un fossato di scolo
un pozzo
per l'acqua piovana
mettere il palo dritto
per sostenere
il giovane albicocco
e il tempo che passa
enumerarlo, scandirlo
senza rifargli il trucco.

Nelle tue mani
c'è un sole
non troppo luminoso
ma chiaro e necessario
che calmo si addormenta
nella sua luce opaca.

Non aggiungi altro
già metti in moto
corri a dare alle viti
l'acqua ramata.

STICK TO JUST a few things, you whisper
and I immediately add: commas
yes, perhaps every so often
a few good periods.

To dig
a drainage ditch
a well
for rainwater
stand the stake up straight
to prop up
the young apricot tree
and to reckon
the passing time, to register it
without embellishments.

Inside your hands
is a sun
not too bright
but clear and necessary
that calmly falls asleep
in its opaque light.

Without further ado
you rush out
to give some copper water
to the grapevines.

È COME SE dovessi ricominciare
tutto dall'inizio, dai primi
stentati passi.
Ora lo so e non aspetto altro.
Sì, avrei dovuto capirlo
dieci anni fa
ma forse non potevo.
Però: *meglio tardi che mai,*
non è così che si dice?

Chiederò il vostro aiuto
assidua collaborazione
per non isolarmi di nuovo
dividermi in più parti
nel corpo e nello spirito.

Anche così va bene
si può vivere in silenzio
cambiare in modo brusco
metodo e direzione
tendere a un pensiero calmo e puro.

Farsi più piccoli
per dormire nei nidi degli uccelli
più agili per arrampicarsi sugli alberi
più leggeri per stendersi sui rami
per poi potarli e raccoglierne i frutti.

Più sottili per passare
tra le sbarre dei cancelli.

It's as if I had to start
all over again from the beginning, from the first
hard-won steps.
Now I know and I can't wait.
Yes, I should have understood this
ten years ago
but maybe I couldn't have.
However: *better late than never,*
isn't that what they say?

I will ask for your help
and assiduous collaboration
so as not to isolate myself again
divide myself into several parts
both in body and spirit.

This is fine, too
one can live in silence
abruptly change
method and direction
reach for a calm, pure thought.

One can become smaller
to sleep in birds' nests
more agile, to climb trees
lighter, to stretch out on their branches
and then prune them and gather their fruits.

Thinner in order to fit
through the gate bars.

21

2

THE UNINTENTIONAL EVIL

(Il male inconsapevole, 2005)

Y no soy yo que sufre sino el otro
el mismo mono milenario
que se refleja en el espejo y llora.

It is not I who suffers but the other
the very same thousand-year-old monkey
that looks in the mirror and cries.

JORGE EDUARDO EIELSON

Quasi una laguna

Qui non tornerò più.
Lo ritrova scolpito
sulla pietra affilata
che lenta rotola giù
per la strada allagata.

Sono piedi e mani ad accrescere la voglia
di esistere e non restare bloccati sul ponte
tra persone distanti che non si conoscono
a osservare barche insabbiate all'orizzonte.

Né passioni né lotta
si procede, si aspetta
nemici quasi innocenti
il cielo oggi è una festa
rallegrata dagli uccelli.
L'acqua rotola intorno
e i muscoli delle stelle
s'ingorgano di luce
indefinita e sprovveduta.

Però: ti amo, pensa, e vorrebbe
non essere odiato se non lo dice.

Almost a Lagoon

I won't come back here again.
He finds this engraved
on the sharp rock
that is slowly rolling
down the flooded street.

It is the feet and hands that increase the desire
to exist, not to remain stuck on the bridge
among distant, unacquainted people
peering at the beached boats in the distance.

Neither passion nor struggle
one proceeds, awaits
nearly innocent enemies
today the sky is a feast
delighted by birds.
The water sloshes around
and the stars' muscles
gorge on indefinite
unwary light.

However: I love you, he thinks, and would like
not to be hated if he doesn't say it.

La strategia del sogno

La ribellione consiste nel guardare una rosa
fino a polverizzarsi gli occhi.

ALEJANDRA PIZARNIK

La polvere imprevista dell'onda
annulla la tenacia del silenzio
più simile alla morte che all'erba
cresciuta sui lampioni delle strade.

Al mare le ore procedono meglio
ci si ricopre di salsedine
si mettono le pinne e in pochi
secondi ci si ritrova fuori dal deserto.

Così lo spazio bianco non finisce
nel pozzo dell'inchiostro, prova
ad allungarsi verso il meridione
a infilare i sogni nelle tasche del vento.

La strategia del sogno, fuori dallo spazio
usuale, presa all'arpione, sottratta al buio
è la memoria ripulita dal male. Ora brilla
l'immagine della rosa triturata dal rancore.

The Strategy of Dreams

*Rebellion consists of staring at a rose
until your eyes are pulverized.*

ALEJANDRA PIZARNIK

The unforeseen powder of waves
annuls the tenacity of silence
more akin to death than to the grass
that grows on lampposts.

By the sea the hours pass more smoothly
you get covered in salt
wear flippers and in a matter of seconds
you're out of the desert.

Thus, the white space does not end
in the inkwell, it tries
to stretch out toward the South
to sneak dreams into the wind's pocket.

The strategy of dreams (outside the usual
space, caught on a harpoon, snatched from darkness)
is memory cleansed from evil. Now the image
of the rose pulverized by rancor is shining.

Quello che non merito

Dentro di noi ci sono i pali delle luci
e i segnali abbattuti dal freddo polare
mi tendi la mano a uncino e io l'afferro
mi sollevo appena sulla punta dei piedi.

Più in alto trovo la sabbia e l'allegra
fila delle orme degli uccelli: la scrittura
insonne, vibrante nel rosso delle rose
nelle vene che scoppiano sulla fronte
nei segni dell'abbandono, delle spine
e sotto i cavi gelati perché uso il male
come un piccone, un martello pneumatico.

Affondo nella carne (la mia, la nostra)
in ciò che resta degli occhi, poi smonto
alla svelta muscoli e nervi, fegato e cuore.

What I Do Not Deserve

Within us are light poles
and the signals knocked down by polar cold
you reach out your hooked hand and I grasp it
slightly lifting myself on my toes.

Higher up I found the sand and the cheerful
trail of bird footprints: a sleepless
script, vibrant in the roses' red
in the veins that burst on the forehead
in the signs of neglect, of thorns
and under the frozen cables, because I use evil
like a pickaxe, a jackhammer.

I plunge it in the flesh (mine, ours)
in what remains of the eyes, then quickly
dismantle muscles and nerves, liver and heart.

Con il vetro tra le dita

Pratico i giorni di festa come se nulla fosse
striscia la luce sotto un tappeto di foglie
ed ecco la voragine di ricordi che prendono
fuoco e poi il lunedì il martedì il mercoledì
e via discorrendo. Le attese, sai, non sono
il cimitero che ci assomiglia
nel suo rumore di voci
nelle macchie dorate della morte
strofinate sulla pelle con il vetro tra le dita.

Per questo la mia fermata era già pronta
prima dei vent'anni. Guarda i fari, i bagliori
che cullano e quelli avuti in dono dalla luna.

With Glass Between the Fingers

I practice holidays like nothing happened
the light slithers under a carpet of leaves
and there is the chasm of memories catching
on fire and then Monday Tuesday Wednesday
and so on and so forth. The waits, you know, aren't
the cemetery that resembles us
in its clamor of voices
in the golden stains of death
rubbed on the skin with glass between the fingers.

This is why my stop was already waiting for me
before I turned twenty. Look at the headlights, the glows
that rock us and those bestowed on us by the moon.

L' ospite

C'era un morto nel letto ma io non lo conoscevo
e lui non conosceva me e forse lui nemmeno
conosceva sé stesso
perché i morti non sanno mai di essere morti
come noi, talvolta, non sappiamo di essere vivi.

Più volte a muso duro gli dissi di andarsene
di togliersi di mezzo ma quello non rispose
aprì soltanto l'occhio sinistro
per rotearlo da una parte e dall'altra.
Mi osservava come se fossi un matto
un mostro o il male allo stato puro, perfetto.
A un certo punto fui stufo e gli gridai: ehi, amico
te ne stai nel mio letto e fai anche lo sguardo brutto?

               Pesava molto
                portato via
               in un sacco.

The Guest

There was a dead man in my bed but I didn't know him
and he didn't know me and perhaps not even
himself
because the dead don't know they are dead
just like we, sometimes, don't know we are living.

Many times I brutally told him to leave
to get out of my way but he wouldn't answer
he merely opened his left eye
to roll it this way and that.
He examined me as if I were a madman
a monster, or evil in its pure and perfect state.
Until I got tired and yelled: hey friend
you're lying in my bed and have the gall to give me a dirty look?

He was heavy
when I carried him off
in a sack.

Un sorso di aceto

Da mesi ritocco la tela che scuote
emozioni da secoli date per disperse
gli alberi dalle foglie dipinte di profilo
le guerre stellari che occultano le stelle.

Avevo sete e ho bevuto il tuo aceto
il peccato era immobile in un fosso
arso il fitto bosco di croci
attutito il sibilo devastante del rimorso.

Sulla notte non aggiungo altro.
Mi riconosco dall'odore umido
dal latte nero munto dal passato
dall'infanzia avuta o sognata
o quella dei figli che ti restano
accanto e scalzi ballano sul cuore:
lo scavano, lo riempiono di suoni.
Poi li ascolto corrermi dentro
frantumare il male con le mani e lo sguardo.

Per questo quando scrivo cancello le parole.

A Sip of Vinegar

For months I've been touching up the canvas
that shakes up emotions deemed lost for centuries
the trees with the leaves painted in profile
the stellar wars that blot out the stars.

I was thirsty and drank your vinegar
as sin lay still in a ditch
the wood thick with crosses—burned
the devastating whistle of regret—muffled.

About the night I won't add anything else.
I recognize myself from the damp smell,
from the black, freshly drawn milk, from the past
from the childhood I had or dreamt
or from that of the children who are still
beside you, dancing over your heart:
digging into it, filling it up with sounds.
Then I listen as they chase after me
and shatter evil with their hands and gaze.

This is why I erase the words as I write.

3

COLUMBIAN MAPS

(*Mappe colombiane*, 2007)

Cada esperanza tiene su memoria,
su sol de hierro, su llanto de exilio.

Every hope has its memory
its sun of iron, its cry of exile.

GIOVANNI QUESSEP

Oggi ho la mia
lieve speranza
tu la tua polpa
la buccia calda.

Il frutto tropicale
divoriamo con calma
operiamo nel bene
con la voce e le dita.

Inutile incontrarci
ridere, stare assieme
se dalla bocca
sputiamo solo fiele.

La flessuosità della palma
si riflette nei passi:
sugli occhi strofina la notte
sulla pelle spalma il suo miele.

TODAY I HAVE my
feeble hope
you your pulp
the warm skin.

The tropical fruit
we calmly devour
we operate for good
with voice and fingers.

It is pointless to meet
to laugh, to be together
if we only spit bile
from our mouths.

The sinuosity of the palm tree
is reflected in our steps:
the night rubs our eyes
spreads its honey over our skin.

GIUGNO è il mese più bello
lo gridano i colori
l'intensa notte equatoriale
con il verdeggiante rumore.

L'infanzia la trovi per strade
di mani tenere, ma coraggiose
perché di rovi e ortiche
più non hanno alcun timore.

L' arazzo delle stelle
snuda la schiena
impervia delle Ande.
Ho bisogno di un flusso
discreto di carezze
di questa luna audace
che arrossa il buio
calma i colpi del cuore
rafforza la memoria
dona allegria alla voce

e al pianto dell'esilio.

June is the finest month
the colors scream it
the intense equatorial night
with its verdant noise.

Childhood is found on the streets
made of hands tender yet brave
because no longer afraid
of thorns or nettles.

The arras of the stars
unsheathes the impervious
back of the Andes.
I'm in need of a discreet flow
of caresses
of this bold moon
that reddens darkness
calms the heart's blows
strengthens memory
bestows good cheer on the voice

and on the cry of exile.

TEMO PER l'anima dell'uomo
per la nostra ombra invisibile
smarrita o prigioniera
di deboli raggi lunari:
faticano ad arrivare al suolo
scaldare corpi, svagati pensieri.

Difficile ravvisare il futuro
anche se passa a un metro di distanza
se sfilano i popoli divisi da un muro
o per via degli ordigni esplosivi
la polvere che si alza verso il cielo
i corpi assassinati da chi si ammazza.

    Restano le pulsioni
    il sangue della foresta
    che ora scorre veloce
    qui, in Sudamerica
    e la voglia di conoscenza
    che da giorni ci spinge
    a seguire le tracce
    del sogno, e a fare festa.

I FEAR for the soul of man
for our invisible shadow
stranded or held captive
by weak moonbeams:
they struggle to reach the ground
to warm up bodies and distracted thoughts.

It is difficult to glimpse the future
though it may pass three feet from you
if peoples parade separated by walls
the dust rising to the sky
from explosive devices
the bodies destroyed by people bent on slaughter.

    The drives are still there
    the forest's blood
    now flowing fast
    here, in South America
    and the thirst for knowledge
    that has been pushing us for days now
    to follow the trail
    of dreams, and to celebrate.

La parola disfa le foglie
tesse abilmente
un manto di germogli
nasconde i tetti rossi
li copre di lune e di stelle.

Per il legno sottratto
la foresta oggi ha le doglie
lascia che tronchi e rami
suonino a lungo
come gigantesche grancasse.

Al mattino un raggio filante
irriga le dure cortecce
di alberi sempreverdi
disegna isolati villaggi
impervi sentieri sulle Ande.

Words undo the leaves
cleverly weave
a mantle of sprouts
hide the red roofs
cover them in moons and stars.

Because of the stolen wood
today the forest has labor pains
and lets its trunks and branches
issue long sounds
as gigantic bass drums.

In the morning a stringy ray
irrigates the tough bark
of the evergreens
sketches isolated villages
impervious trails in the Andes.

LE MASCHERE d'oro
degli antichi sciamani
se ne stanno nascoste
sul fondo del lago.

E il lago si nasconde
nelle maschere d'oro.

THE GOLDEN masks
of ancient shamans
are quietly hiding
at the bottom of the lake.

And the lake is hidden
in the golden masks.

Non sono l'alba
né l'erba
alta che al vento
si piega
e assottiglia la luce.

Né il ramo che sfiora
l'acqua lenta
di un fiume sotterraneo
né l'ombra
segreta che unisce
e frantuma le stanze
della casa rimasta vuota.

La speranza tiene per mano
gli uomini e non li fa
sprofondare nell'oceano.

I AM NOT the dawn
nor the tall
grass that bends
in the wind
and thins out the light.

Nor the branch that skims
the slow water
of an underground river
nor the secret
shadow that connects
and shatters the rooms
of the house left empty.

Hope holds humans
by the hand, doesn't let them
sink into the ocean.

Le cose (gli oggetti. Tipo: la pipa
l'orologio da polso, la lampada
i sandali neri, il telo da spiaggia
persino l'ombrellone) ci spiano
lo sai e rivelano il diritto
di non esistere o di confondersi
nel silenzio degli anni che verranno.

La giusta distanza tra noi e gli oggetti
(la panca su cui siedi, il quaderno,
la penna, le poesie lette e ascoltate,
l'oceano che si riflette nei tuoi occhi,
l'aria umida e calda dell'Amazzonia)
la trovi nel vento che sospinge
la pazienza più avanti. È una ruota
che traccia le curve della memoria
i rapporti provvisori e confusi
quell'offrirsi in mille pezzi per poi
isolarsi ancora e perdersi nella storia.

Come busti privi di braccia
in soffitta dietro i ritratti
polverosi degli avi o in alto
conservati in una cassa di zinco.

THINGS (Objects. For instance: the pipe
the wristwatch, the lamp
the black sandals, the beach towel
even the umbrella) spy on us
(you know they do) and reveal the right
not to exist or to blend
into the silence of future years.

The right distance between us and objects
(the bench you sit on, the notebook,
the pen, the poems read and listened to,
the ocean reflected in your eyes,
the warm and humid air of the Amazon)
you find it in the wind that pushes
patience further on. It is a wheel
that traces the curves of memory
the temporary, confused relationships
offering oneself up in a thousand pieces
only to withdraw again and get lost in history.

Like armless busts sitting
in the attic behind the ancestors'
dusty portraits or preserved
on the top shelf in a zinc box.

OGNI speranza
ogni singolo gesto
adagio si riversa
nelle mappe segrete
trae la sua forza
la sua soffice luce
dallo sguardo del sole.

Per questo l'esilio
può tramutarsi
in sogno senza sosta
in un lungo tragitto
o nel sangue che scorre
e di padre in figlio
passa fluido e sicuro.

Every hope
every single gesture
slowly pours
into secret maps
draws its strength
its soft light
from the sun's gaze.

This is why exile
can transform
ceaselessly in dream
into a long journey
or in the blood that runs
smoothly and confidently
from father to son.

4

TIBER IN FLAMES

(*Tevere in fiamme*, 2008)

La poesía cruza la tierra sola,
apoya su voz en el dolor del mundo
y nada pide – ni siquiera palabras.

Poetry roams the earth in solitude,
rests its voice upon the world's pain
and asks for nothing – not even words

EUGENIO MONTEJO

Di notte la vita ha frammenti di bellezza
nascosti nelle voci suadenti delle foglie
quando si staccano dai rami e lente
planano sull'asfalto, sui sacchi di immondizia.

Da qui vedo il paese, in alto sulla destra
lo stesso che ha scolpito questo cuore
fitto di oscure macchie e pietra grezza
che cede alla polvere i petali della sua pigrizia.

Il fischio vibrante delle canne è spronato
dal vento che trascina con sé le tracce
di fiumi asciutti, o in fiamme,
di territori assetati e sconvolti in questi giorni.

Ora mi lascio sfoltire dall'erba
con gli occhi chiusi poto i ciliegi
ma l'esodo dalle ferite è il frutto che ci afferra
e alimenta la voglia di ripartire dall'inizio
perché la bocca ha le sue aguzze spine
a sigillare i ricordi, i fiori carnosi della savana.

At night life possesses fragments of beauty
hidden in the leaves' mellow voices
when they fall off the trees and slowly
land on the asphalt, or on the bags of garbage.

From here I see the village, above on the right
the same that sculpted this heart of mine
dense with dark stains and rough stone
that yields to dust the petals of its indolence.

The reeds' vibrating whistle is spurred on
by the wind trailing the footprints
of rivers, dried up or in flames, the footprints
of the thirsty lands being ravaged in these days.

Now I let the grass thin me out
eyes closed, I prune the cherry trees
but the exodus from hurt is the fruit that seizes us
and nourishes the longing to begin anew
because the mouth is equipped with sharp thorns
to seal memories, the savannah's fleshy flowers.

Di più non posso sottrarmi alle tenebre
all'abisso, nel mare chiuso in uno specchio
e scalzo andare incontro al figlio. Se potessi
parlarti ti racconterei ogni cosa: il frullio
del pappagallo chiuso in una gabbia
in un salotto ingombro di sbadigli
i toni aspri del cielo che annientano la luce.

Quello non era un sogno ma realtà spalmata
nello sguardo, con le scarpe coperte di fango
i tacchi sbattuti sulle pietre. Ci arpiona
la nuvola che sorvola i giorni e con dolcezza
strappa via la pelle, i grani del rosario.
Di notte diamo fuoco alla città e al bosco
guarda, adesso persino il Tevere è in fiamme!

I can no longer escape the darkness
the abyss, in the sea locked in a mirror
and walk barefoot toward my son. If I could
touch you I'd tell you everything: the fluttering
of the caged parrot in a living room
cluttered with yawns, the harsh tones
of the sky that annihilate the light.

That wasn't a dream but a reality smeared
over your gaze, shoes covered in mud
heels beaten on the stones. We are hooked
by the cloud that soars over the days
and gently rips our flesh, the rosary beads.
At night we set fire to the city and the woods.
Look, now even the Tiber is in flames!

UCCELLI NOTTURNI mettono il becco nel bianco
degli occhi (lasciano un segno di ali leggere)
nei rientri in punta di piedi, nei ricordi
prosciugati dal sale, negli uomini dallo sguardo
onesto, nel regolare scorrere delle stagioni
nei nidi di grano, nelle spighe e nei frutti
nel fumo grigio che sale dalla legna che arde
nel piacere del corpo rivestito di borchie dorate.

Mi rivolgo al caldo tropicale per il piacere
della luce, al brusio emanato dal sordo che ascolta
il sole, all'abilità del sarto che a occhi chiusi ricuce
tagli, al tremore dell'animale dalle zampe legate
al collo. Corpi stesi, martoriati
dalle rovine dei palazzi abbattuti dalle bombe.
Il passaggio di piume ha messo in fuga il caldo
torrido, nel petto resta solo lo scalpitìo dei puledri.

Night birds stick their beaks in the white
of the eyes (leaving a mark of light wings)
in the returns home on tiptoe, in the memories
drained by salt, in the men with the honest
gaze, in the normal passing of seasons
in the nests of wheat, in the spikes and fruits
in the gray smoke rising from the burning wood
in the pleasure of a body clad in golden studs.

I turn to the tropical heat for the pleasure
of its light, to the buzz emanated by the deaf
as they listen to the sun, to the skill of the tailor
mending rips with his eyes closed, to the quivering
of the animal with its legs tied to its neck. Stretched out
bodies, martyred in the rubble of bombed buildings.
The flight of feathers has scattered the torrid
heat, only the pawing of colts survives in the chest.

Tra le fiamme

La scrittura abiura le parole, ravviva il fuoco e piega i fogli in quattro per imbucarli verso destinazioni sconosciute. Non aspettarsi nulla dal sacco aviotrasportato. Da te ho avuto in dono una salda freddezza e qualche sonoro schiaffo ma perdura il profilo del paese, l'argento degli ulivi. Non sono venuto qui per dirti *addio* ma, visto che ci sono, ne approfitto: inseguo un gioco maldestro, fuggo dal dormiveglia, dal tempo che ringhia alle stelle. Raccolgo le gocce distillate dagli abbagli, le azioni di genitori intravisti nell'ombra: i supplizi erano scherzi innocenti? Però il dolore era vero e lo sento ancora scorrermi tra le dita, sulla pelle che brucia.

A forza di pensarti da qui non posso
non vederti ossessiva e nuda
nemmeno sognarti, come non dovrei:
non varrebbe la pena visto che hai
gli occhi spietati e affogati nell'odio.

Sai che i fantasmi trascrivono storie
si caricano il passato sulle spalle
dal fondo del fiume estraggono ghiaia
e marmo, antichi busti romani.
Tra le fiamme ora scorrono zattere d'acqua.

Amid the Flames

Writing abjures the words, rekindles the fire, folds the sheets four ways and mails them to unknown destinations. Don't expect anything from the airborne sack. You have gifted me a firm coldness and a few loud slaps, yet the town's outline endures, the silver of olive trees lives on. I have not come to say *goodbye*, but while I'm at it, I might as well: I play a bumbling game, run from half-sleep, from time growling at the stars. I gather the drops distilled by dazzles, the acts of parents half-seen in the darkness: were those torments but innocent pranks? Yet the pain was real and to this day I feel it run through my fingers, down my scalded skin.

> The more I think of you from here
> the more I see you obsessive and naked
> and dream of you, as I should not:
> what is the point of seeing your pitiless
> eyes drowning in hatred?

> You know that ghosts transcribe stories
> load the past on their backs
> draw gravel from the river floor
> as well as the marble of ancient Roman busts.
> Now water rafts flow amid the flames.

Senza gloria mi piego per raccogliere
i granelli di polvere che ci riconoscono.
Agli occhi appenderò il sorriso e la rabbia,
non mi chiederò se dormo o son desto
e se la notte è solo un residuo di luce
o se questa gioia è il nostro umile concerto.
Una grancassa le dita sul tuo corpo, la lingua
era un violino che slegava ogni dubbio
coi baci volevo strapparti all'esilio, al dolore.

Verranno lune più rosse? Altre pietre?
Ci sorrideranno fiumi più limpidi
terre da arare e difendere a denti stretti.
Indosso le tue parole che un giorno
mi coprirono di bruma calda e protettiva.
Ora che non ci sei ti mostrerò altre rose
farò i conti con gli osti, i vivi e i morti
col vento che culla le foglie e con dolcezza
sospinge, tra sole e luna, lo sposo e la sposa.

WITHOUT GLORY I bend to gather
the grains of dust that recognize us.
On the eyes I will hang the smile and the anger,
will not wonder if I am asleep or awake
whether the night is but a residue of light
or whether this joy is our humble concert.
My fingers on your body were a bass drum
my tongue a violin untying every doubt
with kisses I wished to wrest you from exile, from pain.

Will we see redder moons? Different rocks?
Clearer rivers will smile to us
new lands to plow and guard with clenched teeth.
I wear your words, which once
covered me with a warm and protective haze.
Now that you are gone I will show you more roses
I will settle my scores with the living and the dead
with the wind that cradles the leaves and kindly
urges on, between sun and moon, the bride and the groom.

La città ci rovina addosso, non bastano le palafitte
né il verde della savana. Ai tropici fa freddo
e a volte cade persino la neve.
Sotto i ponti ho visto le tenebre, le croci,
il fiume tagliato in due dall'oceano dei liquami
un tatuaggio di nubi sulla pelle vellutata delle lucertole.

Crolla addosso la pioggia di settembre
i conflitti sul lavoro con le scimmie ammaestrate
i pugni allo stomaco dati e ricevuti
la manciata di chiodi che segnano il percorso
gli alberi strappati alla terra, le menti telecomandate.

 La ripresa del sogno
 perso al volo, in salita
 bagna il becco nel nero delle strade
 nella calma dei buoi che trascinano
 le foglie dei platani, degli ulivi
 persino dei banani dove sta scritta la vita.

Fulmini sul Tevere illuminano gli sfregi sul volto della Terra.
Nel paesaggio saldo e assoluto delle rovine che ci rotolano
addosso trovo un canto e ti vengo incontro (se me lo permetti,
se posso). Nello sguardo la luce tagliente di Roma, sulle
spalle i detriti delle case e questa voce che alla tua si affianca.

giugno 2008

THE CITY comes tumbling down on us, the stilt houses
can't help it, nor the green of the savannah. At the tropics
it's cold and at times it even snows.
Under bridges I have seen darkness, crosses,
the river cut in half by the ocean of sewage
a cloud-shaped tattoo on the velvety skin of lizards.

The September rain comes crashing down
the workplace rows with trained monkeys
the gut punches dealt and received
the handful of nails that mark the journey
the uprooted trees, the remote-controlled minds.

    The recovery of the dream
    lost in flight, on the climb
    wets its beak in the black of streets
    in the calm of oxen dragging
    the leaves of plane and olive trees
    even banana trees, on which life is written.

Lightning over the Tiber lights up the gashes on the Earth's
face. In the firm, absolute landscape of the ruins rolling down
on us I find a song and walk toward you (if you will allow me,
if I may). In my gaze Rome's cutting light, on my shoulders the
rubble of houses and this voice of mine coming up beside yours.

June 2008

Di notte fodero il buio con spessi strati di fango
e affascinato ascolto le cicale che da sempre
ci respirano accanto o si rifugiano nelle vene.
Così resisto al tempo, triste ma non sconfitto
la testa con le spine e dai canini sgorga il veleno.
Nel flusso del sogno c'era sangue dappertutto
di genitori che in guerra hanno perso un figlio.

Rivivo il viaggio dell'indeciso, del pazzo o ubriaco
trafitto da foglie di banano, platano e fico.
Talvolta osservo a occhi chiusi come avrei voluto
che fosse il mondo, ascolto il crepitio del forno
carezzo e annuso il morbido pane, i decenni
spesi a difendersi dal nemico, a lanciare
appigli e frasi di conforto alle navi in fuga di Ulisse.

AT NIGHT I upholster the dark in thick coats of mud
and enthralled listen to the cicadas that breathe beside us
since time immemorial or take shelter in the veins.
Thus I stand up to time, sad but not defeated
with thorns on my head and poison gushing from my canines.
In the dream's flow there was blood everywhere
the blood of parents who have lost a son in the war.

I relive the journey of the undecided, the madman or the drunkard
pierced through by the leaves of banana, plane or fig trees.
Sometimes I observe with eyes closed the world
I had wished for, listen to the crackle of the oven
caress and smell the soft bread, the decades spent
fighting off the enemy, throwing footholds
and comforting words to Ulysses' fleeing ships.

5

THE RIVER IN THE SEA

(*Il fiume nel mare*, 2010)

to those who died crossing the Mediterranean Sea
looking for a home
looking for work

Primero estaba el mar. Todo estaba oscuro. No había sol, ni luna, ni gente, ni animales, ni plantas. Sólo estaba la madre mar. Y ella era agua y agua por todas partes. Era río, laguna, quebrada y mar. Así ella estaba en todo lugar. La madre no era gente, ni nada, ni cosa alguna. Ella era Aluna. Era espíritu de lo que iba a venir y era pensamiento y memoria.

First there was the sea. Everything was dark. There was no sun, no moon, no people, no animals, no plants. There was only mother sea. And she was water and water everywhere. She was river, lagoon, ravine and sea. Thus, she was everywhere. Mother was not a person, or a thing, she was no thing. She was Aluna. She was the spirit of what was to come, she was thought and memory.

KOGI MYTHOLOGY

Il FIUME fa ben poco
per sottrarci al male
inconsapevole
all'aridità dei giorni
al piombo nero
che ci trafigge
però conserva in sé
da sempre il giusto
necessario tepore
ne fa scorta
ed aspetta paziente
di metterlo negli occhi
dei candidi uccelli marini
di donarlo a chi percorre
al buio il Mediterraneo
per proteggere i figli
dai morsi della fame
e scavare nel sogno
un'umile abitazione
un lavoro sereno, sicuro.

Quante mani vuote di appigli
quanti corpi fluttuanti
in attesa di sparire nel fondo.

THE RIVER does little
to protect us
from unintentional evil
from the day's dryness
from the black lead
that pierces us
yet it has always retained
in itself the right
necessary warmth
stockpiled it
and awaited patiently
to put it in the eyes
of the white sea birds
to gift it to those who cross
the Mediterranean Sea
in darkness to protect their children
from the pangs of hunger
to build in their dreams
a humble abode
a fair, secure job.

So many hands without a handhold
so many floating bodies
waiting to disappear into the bottom.

IN CROCE i corpi a un metro dall'acqua
braccia tagliate, impilate da una parte.
Schiacciati, con incisi nomi cuori date
frasi oscene, disumane. Le facce gonfie
con bruciature sul collo gambe costato.
Come se non fossero uomini
con le loro mogli e madri, i giovani figli
ma esche buone per la morte e il dolore.

Il volto gonfio, il collo tirato, le mani
attaccate alle reti: la fuga, poi il naufragio
nell'eroica attraversata del Mediterraneo.
Corpi utilizzati per un falò, probabilmente
arsi con l'impegno di non soffrire *mai più*
di fame, di lavoro perché per loro non c'è
una casa di mattoni né tantomeno di cristallo.

Resta alla fine soltanto il silenzio
dei morti sepolti, giù in fondo al mare.

THE BODIES in a cross shape three feet
from the water, arms cut and piled on one side.
Crushed, engraved with names, hearts, dates,
obscene, inhuman phrases. The faces swollen
with burns over the neck, legs, ribcage.
As if these weren't men
with their wives and mothers, their young children
but mere baits good for death and pain.

The face swollen, the neck drawn, the hands
clinging to the nets: the escape, then the shipwreck
in the heroic crossing of the Mediterranean Sea.
Bodies utilized for a bonfire, probably
burnt with the commitment to suffer *no more*
from hunger, from joblessness as there are no
brick houses for them, let alone crystal ones.

Only silence remains in the end
from the dead buried at the bottom of the sea.

Si sopravvive anche a questo
tanto le parole enunciate
sono di cartastraccia
asole chiuse col filo spinato
così dopo non passa
l'aria e si sta più caldi anche se
c'è vergogna per quest'essenza
metallica che ci diminuisce
slega e allontana gli uni dagli altri.

Si sopravvive ai ponti che crollano
ai passaggi segreti murati dal tempo
si comincia a credere a futuri ricordi
si sta davanti al quadro bianco:
con calma lo si riempie con lo sguardo
di colori scuri, di segni primitivi
di sogni astratti che non valgono molto.

 Poi, ecco le case
 che franano nel fiume.

WE END UP outliving this, too
besides, the words spoken
are made of scrap paper
eyelets sewn shut with barbed wire
so that no air goes through
and we are all a bit warmer although
there is shame over this metallic
essence that diminishes us
unties and removes us from each other.

We outlive the collapsed bridges
the secret passageways walled off by time
we begin to believe in future memories
we stand before the white painting
and calmly fill it in with our gaze
adding dark colors, primitive markings
abstract dreams of little worth.

> Then, here are the houses
> collapsing into the river.

HAI UN volto di bambino ribelle, scontroso, a volte
di ragazzo che in un soffio ha bruciato la giovinezza.
L' onda che viene a travolgerci è il vento che brama
il nostro spirito e veloce lo trasforma in pulviscolo
il sogno in statua di gesso impassibile alla tormenta.

Mare
mare grosso
mare neonato
mare verde smeraldo
mare di processioni secolari
mare che viene da alte montagne
mare che congiunge i litorali del mondo
mare che vorrebbe raccontare il suo amore
mare che si gonfia e distrugge la costa e i villaggi
mare che conosce Itaca e prega per il ritorno negato
mare che demolisce e si attorciglia alle tue piccole dita
spruzzi d'acqua salata sul tuo volto di bambino spettinato.

Osservi ancora con la bocca semichiusa
al di là dell'orizzonte che separa la morte dalla vita. Ora
non ti va di pensare, al bene e al male che assieme verranno.

You HAVE the face of a surly, rebellious child, at times
the face of a boy who has burnt out his youth in a whiff.
The wave about to wash us away is the wind that longs for
our spirit and quickly turns it into fine dust
our dream into a statue of plaster impervious to the storm.

Sea
swollen *sea*
newborn sea
emerald-green *sea*
sea of secular processions
sea that comes from tall mountains
sea that connects the world's coasts
sea that would like to tell of its love
sea that swells and destroys the coast and villages
sea that knows Ithaca and prays for the denied return
sea that demolishes and wraps around your little fingers
sprays of saltwater on your unkempt child's face.

You peer again with your mouth half-closed
beyond the horizon that separates death from life. Now
you don't feel like thinking, about the good and bad that will
come together.

Ho ATTESO una risposta
nel frattempo ho avuto
paura per te, e per noi.

Forse per questo il volto
della statua che contiene
i nostri destini è esploso.

In schegge d'acqua salata
in frantumi di verità
che ora affondano il mare.

I HAVE WAITED for an answer
meanwhile I have feared
for you, for us.

Perhaps this is why the face
of the statue that contains
our fates has shattered.

Into shards of saltwater
into shreds of truth
which are now sinking the sea.

PER GIORNI fiutiamo il profumo
rincorso per oltre trent'anni
e allora ci assale la voglia
di remare da soli controcorrente
nutrirsi di alghe, ridurre il ritmo
farsi da parte
e con le dita spegnere le fiamme.

Poi mostrare con calma alle sirene
le distanze tracciate
col sangue sulle mappe solitarie.

For days we have been sniffing the scent
we chased for thirty years
and now the longing seizes us
to row alone against the current
feed on algae, slow the rhythm
move aside
and put out the fire with our fingers.

And then calmly show the sirens
the distances we covered
in blood on our solitary maps.

Ti specchi e non sai cosa dirti
conti gli occhi i nasi le bocche
attorcigliate al fuoco, alle lingue
le mani legate per non agire
per non ritrovarti di nuovo
a scolpire porte e finestre
con le unghie e poi a sbattere la testa
contro un muro di lava incandescente.

Sotto di noi ci sono giardini assopiti
se scavi trovi la terra fredda ma grassa
buona per seminare il grano
o far crescere gli ulivi e la vite
e poi un lago, la piazza con l'angelo
di bronzo dalle ali spalancate e, infine,
la strada che conduce alla città sepolta
ai ruderi avvinghiati alle radici del bosco.

You LOOK in the mirror and don't know what to say
to yourself, count the eyes, noses, mouths
tangled up in fire, in tongues
hands tied in order not to act
not to end up again
sculpting doors and windows
with your fingernails then hitting your head
against a wall of incandescent lava.

Underneath us are dozing gardens
if you dig you'll find the earth cold but rich
good for sowing wheat
or growing olive trees and grapevines
then a lake, the piazza with the bronze
spread-winged angel, and then at last
the road leading to the buried city
to the ruins clinging to the forest's roots.

L'ACQUA DEL mare pulisce le rocce
con le impronte, il volto, le labbra.
Non ci sono gli applausi delle sirene
ma l'umore dell'onda rende il silenzio
soffice schiuma, l'*io* isolato e il *noi*
annoiato. Conto le ore che ci separano
dalla maschera da indossare di nuovo
tornando, tra qualche giorno, al lavoro.

Al di là degli scogli ammicca l'occhio
intermittente del faro:
lo raggiungeremo a nuoto, prima o poi.

THE SEAWATER cleans the rocks
with fingerprints, face, and lips
There is no applause from the sirens
but the wave's mood turns the silence
into soft foam, the isolated *I*,
the bored *we*. I'm counting the hours until
we must wear our mask again
in a few days, when we go back to work.

Beyond the rocks there winks
the intermittent eye of the lighthouse:
we will reach it by swimming, sooner or later.

6

IN THE WOLF'S GAZE

(*Nello sguardo del lupo*, 2014)

to Flavia e Simone

*Biti moraš odprt
kakor rana,
ker pravo ime stvari
je skrito*

You have to be open
like a wound,
because the true name of things
is hidden

KAJETAN KOVIČ

È GIÀ NOTTE e il pallido chiarore lunare fonde
la corteccia dei noci che da qui si possono
solo intravedere, svelto lo sguardo vaga
per conto suo in cerca di luoghi solitari
di spazi dove fuggire e afferrarsi, di nascoste
costellazioni che spiano gli ululati della Terra.

Il buio di faville stellari è già un miracolo.
L'ansia s'inarca, scorre un groviglio di stelle
l'invisibile movimento di altri sistemi solari.
La luce sgrana le tenebre, dilaga l'effluvio
dell'erba e il buio deflagra allo schiudersi
del giorno. Nel plumbeo cielo di Roma
il vento si blocca e piccoli esseri filiformi
planano sul tetto: stanchi crollano all'istante
pensando ai pianeti in fuga, ai lupi da accudire.
All'alba corrono allegri sui palmi delle mie mani.

It's ALREADY nighttime and the pale moonlight melts
the bark off the walnut trees that can only
be glimpsed from here, quickly the gaze roams
on its own, looking for lonely places
for spaces to flee and cling to, for hidden
constellations spying on the Earth's howling.

The darkness of stellar flickers is already a miracle.
Anxiety arches up, a tangle of stars drifts by
the invisible movement of other solar systems.
Light frays the night, the effluvium of grass
expands and darkness explodes as the day
breaks. In the lead gray Roman sky
the wind abates and small spindly creatures
land on the roof: tired, they instantly collapse
thinking of the escaping planets, of wolves that need tending.
At dawn they run merrily over the palm of my hands.

CHINO GLI OCCHI e assorbo la linea del paese
vago nel profumo del bosco, tra le tue rose.
I pestaggi segreti si scontrano con le labbra
è come se non sapessimo più sognare o dire
e i cerchi di luce arretrano, caricano bagagli:
le vie, i guanti, un altrove, l'ombra rimuove
i sassi e ci s'imbatte in uno spoglio
territorio, si entra in un bar dell'autostrada

ci s'intravede nel fondo del caffè, esplode
lo sfregio all'infanzia. CASTELLO CHIUSO
PER RESTAURO, nel museo le anfore, i vasi
recuperati negli abissi e nel Mediterraneo
i pesci che vegliano i morti in cerca
di una casa, di un lavoro. *Nulla è cambiato*
da mesi attendo un aiuto per disfare i grovigli.
Non parlo scrutando le onde, il porto che crolla.

I LOWER MY EYES to absorb the line of the countryside
I wander in the scent of woods, among your roses.
Secret beatings collide with lips
it's as if we don't know how to dream or say anymore
and the rings of light recede, take on baggage:
the streets, the gloves, an elsewhere, the shadow removes
the rocks and we bump into a bare
territory, we walk into a roadside coffee bar

we half-see each other at the far end of the café
the affront to childhood explodes. CASTLE CLOSED
FOR RESTORATION, in the museum the amphora, the vases
wrested from the depths, and in the Mediterranean
the fish keeping vigil over the dead in search
of a house, a job. *Nothing has changed*
for months I've been seeking help in undoing the tangles.
I don't talk as I peer over the waves, the crumbling harbor.

I FIORI ululano di notte e al volo
afferrano le stelle quei lamenti
e nell'abisso sfrecciano comete.
Rifare il trucco all'infanzia negata?
Fatti da parte che vado di fretta
tardi per dirne, per cambiare strada.
Per l'ira la sedia saltò sul tetto
del mio peso non volle più saperne.
Ora la traccia è quella del lupo
lento gli vado dietro mentre dorme.

FLOWERS howl at night and at once
the stars seize on those laments
and comets shoot into the abyss.
Should we give our denied childhood a makeover?
Get out of my way I am in a hurry
too late to talk about it, to change direction.
Out of anger the chair jumped on the roof
it was fed up with my weight.
Now it's the wolf's tracks
I slowly pursue him while he sleeps.

LE ZONE OSCURE recitano un ruolo
codardo ideato dalle illusioni.
Nascondere ciò che ci nutre?
La salvezza è in quest'amore
sopravvissuto a luoghi di tortura.
Figli mordono padri che non sanno
giocare. L' eros azzoppato e l'attesa
dell'alba legata al corpo, alla carne
così il tempo disperso nella luce
è assediato dalla tela del ragno.

Dark zones play a cowardly role
conceived by illusions.
Must we hide what nourishes us?
Salvation is in this love
that has survived the places of torture.
Sons bite fathers who can't play.
The hamstrung eros and the wait
for dawn tied to the body, to the flesh
thus time lost in light
is besieged by the spider's web.

Dove incontrarci? Il mistero ci tende
la mano amputata: non siamo pronti.
Sul filo spinato uccelli dai becchi
torti mettono ali ad asciugare: se scrivi
non ti fermi e non pensi. Se non pensi
scrivi, se scrivi rinasci. Facile, se solo
ci fosse lei e uno strato di candida neve.
Mia figlia teneva l'ombrello, io lavoravo
sotto la pioggia, adesso fatico a parlarci:
l'azzurro del suo sguardo divora i discorsi.

WHERE to meet? Mystery offers us
its amputated hand: we are not ready.
On the barbed wire birds with crooked beaks
are hanging wings to dry: if you write
you don't stop nor think. If you don't think
you write, if you write you are reborn. Easy if
only she were there, and a layer of pure white snow.
My daughter held the umbrella as I worked
in the rain, now I have a hard time talking to her
the blue from her gaze devours speech.

Non riuscivo a muovere un passo
da giorni a Madrid e non lo sapevo.
Con un dolore alla schiena, colpito
dal fiasco delle nostre aspettative.
Tirano su... una cassa le tue storie.
La morte adora chi pesca nel fondo.
La brezza t'ingigantisce la bocca.
Sono un visionario ma sono vere
le menzogne. Ridi e di te, di nuovo
m'innamoro. *Quando la prima volta?*

For days in Madrid I could not take
a single step and I didn't know it.
With pain in my back, struck
by the fiasco of our prospects.
They're digging up... a crate, your stories.
Death adores bottom-fishers.
Your mouth balloons in the breeze.
I am a visionary but the lies are true.
You laugh and I fall in love with you
all over again. *When was the first time?*

OLTRE il recinto un cavallo, lo vidi
esplodermi nella testa. I papaveri
non piangono pur con il sangue
stipato nei sogni, bruciano il buio
e aprono sentieri lontani dalle rose.
A questo punto torniamo all'inizio
alle scarpe chiodate unte dai funghi
all'alba a piazza Navona. Impigliato
nel sonno i fogli sono mongolfiere
ed ali le spine, salvia il pelo sul muso.

Beyond the fence a horse, I saw him
explode in my head. The poppies
don't cry even with all the blood crammed
in dreams, they burn away the darkness
and blaze trails far from the roses.
At this point we're back where we started
at the spiked shoes smeared by mushrooms
in piazza Navona at dawn. Snagged on sleep
the sheets are air balloons, the thorns
are wings, and sage the hair on your snout.

Non voglio l'assoluto, basta e avanza
il tuo sorriso, un'ombra soleggiata.
Tempo scaduto, urlò l'orologiaio
e le lancette giravano svelte
bruciando secoli più che secondi.
Lo scoprì tornando da un triplo sogno
non vedendosi davanti allo specchio.
Cosa fai per amarmi? Io? Nulla, solo
mi affliggo per quello che fummo
per i plastici volteggi dei nostri corpi.

I DON'T WANT the absolute, your smile
is more than enough, a sun-drenched shade.
Time's up, cried the watchmaker
and the hands were spinning fast
burning away centuries rather than seconds.
He found out as he returned from a triple dream
he couldn't see himself in the mirror.
What do you do to love me? Me? Nothing
I only grieve over what we were
over the plastic twirls of our bodies.

7

THE FACE AND THE JOURNEY

(Il volto e il viaggio, 2017)

Ich höre jeden in mir schreiten
und breite meine Einsamkeiten
von Anbeginn zu Anbeginn.

I hear everybody's footfalls
and widen my solitudes
from beginning to beginning.

RAINER MARIA RILKE

Fili stellari

A terra e vorrei buttar via
le cose che non servono:
l'inutile, anche il superfluo.
Seduto al centro della stanza
ma ho sempre troppe cose
da sistemare e poi, per dirla
tutta, è proprio il superfluo
(l'esatta futilità di ogni cosa)
a donare la forza di alzarmi
uscire per strada, incontrare
altre persone e poi inseguire
un sogno dove ai fili stellari
si attorcigliano volti e versi.

Stellar Threads

In the dumps, and I'd like
to throw out the things I don't need:
all that is useless and superfluous.
Sitting in the middle of the room
but I have always too many things
to think about and besides, to be
truthful, it is precisely the superfluous
(the exact futility of everything)
that gives me the strength to get up
to get out in the street, to meet other
people and then to chase
a dream in which stellar threads
intertwine with faces and verse.

La via del ritorno

Restavo incantato a osservare i vascelli
e il limpido cielo, poi c'era il mare
che avvolgeva con delicatezza la spiaggia.
Entro in punta di piedi nei tuoi occhi adulti
scolpiti dal vento e allora arrivano visioni
di un colore rosso cupo, martellato a lungo.
Così stagionano presagi
che nelle vene si sgretolano a rilento.

Non sogno il futuro, non lo conosco
e tuttavia vorrei capirlo, vorrei che fosse
parte di me, di noi, della mia fede. Sono
alte montagne o città d'Europa, fiumi
che scorrono rapidi nel taglio dell'abisso
e mi spavento, allora tu sorridi e io grido
che non posso entrare in questo paesaggio
perché poi non ritroverei la via del ritorno.

The Way Back

Enchanted, I'd observe the vessels
and the clear sky, then the sea
would gently wrap itself around the beach.
I tiptoe into your grownup eyes
sculpted by the wind and I get visions
in a dark red color hammered out at length.
This is how presages age, as they
slowly crumble in our veins.

I don't dream the future, I don't know it
yet I'd like to understand it, I wish
it were a part of me, of us, of my faith. It's
tall mountains or cities of Europe, rivers
running fast through the cut of the abyss
and it scares me, then you smile and I cry
that I can't walk into this landscape
I couldn't find my way back if I did.

L'orizzonte messo di traverso

Cos'è un ricordo? Il tanfo
afferra alla gola resta soltanto
una montagna di rovine.
La fermezza è un vizio
come un altro. Se parli
troppo annulli il silenzio.
Canto le braccia sudate e virili
una lama di luce e arriva il sospetto
che nulla resterà di noi se non l'oblio
del nostro amore, le passate avventure.

Accanto a un lago frugo tra pietre e rovi
in cerca della felicità smarrita, della casa
lievitata nei sogni. Il fuoco divampa
tra le canne e oltre i tetti la luna si spegne.
Fumano i giorni in attesa che il sole spunti
dalla parte giusta e invece appare
un orizzonte sghembo, messo di traverso
che blocca il lento movimento delle stelle.

I salici piangenti lungo il fiume in secca
sono verdi: alla grande se la ridono di noi!

The Horizon Set Aslant

What is a memory? Its stench
seizes by the throat, only a mountain
of ruins remains.
Firmness is a defect
like any other. If you talk too much
you erase silence.
I sing of virile, sweaty arms
a blade of light carries the suspicion
that nothing will remain of us but the oblivion
of our love, of our past adventures.

Beside a lake I rummage through rocks and brambles
for the happiness I lost, for the house leavened
in dreams. Fire blazes among the reeds
and the moon goes out behind the roofs.
The days smoke by waiting for the sun to rise
on the correct side: instead, a crooked
horizon appears, set aslant
against the star's slow journey.

The weeping willows along the dry riverbed
are green: how grandly they mock us!

Nulla ti appartiene

A due passi da un palo arrugginito
ti prepari a un incontro: manterrai
la vivacità del bosco? Rabbioso
ma vuoi rivederla un'ultima volta.
Fiuti radici d'ombra, batti il ritmo
su scaglie di luce e con la mente
esplori le zone più remote del corpo.

Sbuffa la vela ed emergi dall'acqua:
navi bloccate dal sangue fraterno
in Oriente altri scenari di guerra.
Fermo nel traffico sogni l'amore:
unghie, labbra, dita sul volto
nella bocca la sua lingua in fiamme.

«Nulla ti appartiene!»
urla il roditore ben nascosto tra le ossa.

Nothing Belongs to You

Two steps away from a rusty pole
you get ready for a tryst: will you maintain
the vivacity of the woods? Though angry
you want to see her one last time.
You sniff roots of shadow, beat the rhythm
on slivers of light and with your mind
explore the remotest zones of the body.

The sail puffs and you emerge from water:
ships blockaded by fraternal blood
in the East other war scenarios.
Stuck in traffic, you dream of love:
fingernails, lips, fingers on face
in your mouth her tongue in flames.

          "Nothing belongs to you!"
cries the rodent well-hidden amid the bones.

Fili e frammenti

Ho sfiorato la bellezza
senza mai raggiungerla
del tutto. Ed è stato
un modo come un altro
per tirare avanti
pensando alla salute
dei boschi, delle foglie.
L'ho sfiorata, persino
e talvolta mi ha parlato
per vedere tra le nuvole
dissolversi le mie mosse.
Annego ormai da giorni
in un viaggio dell'orrore
senza volto né dimora:
occultarsi, poi scomparire.

Sei un coraggioso perdente che la sconfitta
mai abbandona, adesso devi solo rilassarti.
Nel volto gli occhi chiusi che osservano
ogni cosa pur non vedendo nulla
se non il miraggio della bellezza
se non il bianco dei muri delle case vuote
se non il caldo sole al di là delle montagne
se non il filo di fumo della sigaretta
se non il riflesso della polvere dei nostri giorni.

Threads and Fragments

I've brushed against beauty
without ever being able
to reach it in full. And it's been
a way like any other
to get by
thinking of the health
of the woods, of the leaves.
I've brushed against it, even
and on occasion it has spoken to me
only to see my moves
dissolve among the clouds.
I've been drowning for days
in a horror journey
without a face or a home:
to hide, then to vanish.

You are a courageous loser whom defeat
never abandons, now you just need to relax.
In your face closed eyes that observe
everything though they see nothing
if not the mirage of beauty
if not the white on the walls of empty houses
if not the warm sun beyond the mountains
if not the thread of smoke from a cigarette
if not the reflection of the dust of our days.

Ridere ogni giorno

Conto fino a cento, poi ti sussurro
all'orecchio che amo i tuoi capelli
quando sono in fiamme e ardono
nel mio cuore. Allora il sangue
scorre in senso inverso, nei boschi
si aprono passaggi e nelle pieghe
del male s'infiltrano giovani fiumi
dalle trote argentate che inebriano
l'aria, il respiro. Non ho più il fiato
sul collo, allora il buio si allontana.
Riprendo il dialogo interrotto
pieno di virgole, punti interrogativi.

Pentito di non ridere ogni giorno
mi sforzo di essere migliore: non è
facile, la boria atterra le mie mosse.
Spero di far presto e confessarti
che il blu dei tuoi occhi mi sveglia
se dormo, sbalza il tempo, lo frena
se siamo in uno spazio solo nostro
che non è una disfatta. Ecco, siamo
una cosa sola benché divisi quasi
su tutto, non c'è bisogno di contare
fino a cento oppure a mille prima
di sussurrarti in un orecchio: *ti amo*.

To Laugh Every Day

I count to a hundred, then whisper
in your ear that I love your hair
where it's on fire and burns
within my heart. Then blood
flows backwards, passages open
in woods and the folds of evil
are infiltrated by young rivers
filled with silvery trout that exalt
the air and breath. No one's breathing
down my neck now, so darkness recedes.
I resume the interrupted dialogue
full of commas and question marks.

Feeling guilty of not laughing every day
I strive to be better: it isn't easy
arrogance strikes down my moves.
I hope I'll be quick to confess
that the blue in your eyes awakens me
if I sleep, unhinges time, holds it back
if we are in a space entirely our own
which isn't a defeat. You and I are one
although divided on almost
everything, there's no need to count
to a hundred or even a thousand
before I whisper in your ear: *I love you.*

Uomo in fuga

Queste pagine pesano perché hanno molte
storie da raccontare sulle stelle polverose
maltrattate dal furore del buio.
Era notte fonda quando bussasti alla porta
venni ad aprirti in pigiama con gli occhi
socchiusi. Tornavi da me dopo essere stata
per mesi da lui. Non dissi nulla, forse un
ciao. Ti accolsi con affetto e un abbraccio
bevemmo qualcosa, tu andasti in bagno
dopo facemmo l'amore quasi controvoglia.

Ora ti osservo pelare patate e vedere la tivù
come se fosse normale, come se fosse
una cosa che hai fatto tutti i giorni. Per questo
i minuti pesano parecchio: hanno troppe cose
da dire, troppe storie da raccontare! Meglio
prendere il largo e sparire dalla tua, dalla mia
vita e lasciarti sbucciare patate, giocare
con il telecomando. Tanto la casa è in affitto:
prima o poi dovrai lasciarla e cercarne un'altra
più piccola e meno bella. Ed io sarò già lontano.

Man on the Run

These pages are heavy as they have
so many stories to tell about dusty stars
mistreated by the rage of darkness.
It was the dead of night when you knocked
on my door, I opened in my pajamas, eyes
half-closed. You'd returned to me after
months with him. I said nothing, perhaps
just *hi*. I welcomed you with fondness and a hug
we had a drink, you went to the bathroom
then we made love almost reluctantly.

Now I observe you as you peel potatoes
and watch TV, as if it were normal,
something you did every day. This is why
the minutes weigh heavily: too much
to say, too many stories to tell! Better make
myself scarce, vanish from your life and mine,
let you peel your potatoes, toy with the remote.
Besides, I'm renting here: sooner or later
you'll have to leave this place and find another
smaller and less nice. And I'll be far gone.

Il colpo di grazia

Dal terrazzo guardo un uomo
seduto in un parco: si osserva
i piedi, le scarpe e si sforza
di capire quello che lo circonda
come in attesa del colpo di grazia.

Perché mi dà così pena pensarti?
Ti sei spenta: dovevi essere la luce
che scalda i ricordi. Un fringuello
oltrepassa il filo spinato, lo seguo
con lo sguardo e strappo le foglie
gialle del fico. Ho un volto d'asino
e allo specchio mi raglio contro.
Si fa gelido il frinire dei grilli
e la spada delle tue parole balbetta
come se contemplasse il paesaggio
con i miei occhi. Esistono zone
luminose circondate dal buio e tu
mi hai guidato da quelle parti, mi hai
fatto comprendere la gioia e il dolore.

Come in attesa del colpo di grazia
abbasso la testa e resto seduto
lontano e sereno. Ci sono volti
che puoi vedere soltanto a occhi chiusi.

Coup de Grâce

From the balcony I watch a man
sitting in a park: he's looking
at his feet, his shoes, striving
to make sense of his surroundings
as though awaiting the coup de grâce.

Why does it pain me so to think of you?
You have gone dark: you were supposed to be
the light that warms memories. A finch
flies over the barbed wire, I follow it
with my eyes as I pull the yellow leaves off
the fig tree. I have a donkey's face
and bray at myself in the mirror.
The cricket's chirping turns ice cold
and the sword of your words stutters
as though it admired the landscape
through my eyes. There exist luminous
zones surrounded by darkness and you
have led me through them, have
made me understand both joy and pain.

As if awaiting the coup de grâce
I lower my head and remain seated
faraway and peaceful. There are faces
you can only see with your eyes closed.

Campo minato

Parlavo di me come se fossi un altro
così un ghigno intermittente mi abolì
per sempre. Restai a calcolare i giorni
gli errori, gli amici andati e quelli mai
avuti. Figli, fratelli, genitori. Penavo
come un cane rifiutato, preso a calci
sassate ma ora sono qui in compagnia
di volti in fuga appena conosciuti
e scrivo lettere al nemico, parlo
con gli angeli che sorreggono la Terra.

Ecco la cieca disperazione di una strada ferita
a morte: dov'è la luce? E la calma che trafigge
il rumore? Penso a te stando steso sull'erba
di un campo minato, con le mani azzurre
e la faccia sporca di fumo, le gambe avvolte
di morbido muschio gonfiato dal vento
quel tipo di vento tagliente che regala prodigi.

Minefield

I talked about me as if I were someone else
so an intermittent smirk abolished me
forever. I was left to calculate the days
the errors, the friends I'd lost and the ones
I never had. Children, siblings, parents.
I suffered like a rejected dog, a mutt you kick
or hit with stones, but now I'm here in the
company of faces on the run I just met
and write letters to the enemy, speak
with the angels that hold up the Earth.

Here's the blind desperation of a fatally wounded
street: where is the light? Is it the calm that pierces
noise? I think of you stretched out on the grass
of a minefield, your hands blue and your face
dirty with smoke, your legs wrapped
in soft musk swollen by the wind
that kind of cutting wind that bestows miracles.

Translator's Note

Alessio Brandolini (b. 1958) grew up in Monte Compatri, a village perched on the hilly outskirts of Rome, to a numerous family of modest means. At eleven, he began working in summers and on weekends to contribute to his family's income. He worked as a waiter and a laborer at construction sites, and helped out his father in the field. An old-school farmer and a man of few words, his father related to his children mainly through an ethic of hard work. The rough, ancestral beauty of country life would become a constant motif in Alessio's poetry.

Alessio's coming of age coincided with the period of Italian turmoil known as the Years of Lead (late 1960s to the early 1980s), when warring far-left and far-right factions sought to overthrow the government through acts of political terrorism. Though himself a left-wing activist, Alessio was profoundly distressed by the climate of violence. Unlike many of his like-minded friends, he ultimately refused to see the government as an enemy, and instead of embracing the armed struggle, he became a *carabiniere*. He was twenty-years old when he enlisted, just a few days after the 1978 killing of Aldo Moro by the Red Brigades, arguably the moment of highest tension in those convulsed years. As a left-wing carabiniere, Alessio encountered some discrimination, but for the most part he remembers his years of service as a lesson in courage ("as carabinieri" he pointed out, "we had earned the dubious distinction of getting shot at by both left-wing and right-wing terrorists"), compassion and respect for one's country's institutions. References to this traumatic period of Italian history appear in veiled, highly condensed images throughout his oeuvre.

While in the service, Alessio spent his evenings reading, studying, writing poetry—as had been his habit since adolescence—and contributing to literary magazines. He also attended the Università La Sapienza in Rome, from which he graduated *cum laude* in Modern Italian Literature. After graduating, he won a job as a parliamentary assistant at the Senate, a post which he held until retirement. He has been married for almost forty years and has two children. He resides in Rome, but still maintains the family's plot of land in Monte Compatri.

After winning the prestigious Montale Prize with the poem *L'alba a piazza Navona* (1992), and then the Alfonso Gatto prize with his first collection (*Divisori orientali*, 2002), his literary career was established. Upon the publication of *Poesia della terra* (2004), he became a frequent guest of literary festivals both in Italy and abroad, especially Latin America. His participation in the Poetry festival of Medellín, Colombia was a revelatory experience that would become the basis for his 2007 poetry book *Mappe colombiane*. During his stay in Colombia, Alessio familiarized himself with Spanish, a language whose mastery would eventually allow him to become the assiduous translator and publisher of several Latin American poets in Italy. He had already met important ones at Medellín, such as the Mexican José Emilio Pacheco and the Colombian Juan Manuel Roca—like-minded travel companions whose friendships endures to this day. Alessio was astonished to realize that, in Colombia, poetry is an activity avidly pursued and enjoyed, a vocation ardently discussed by both young and old—unlike in Italy, where it is relegated to a marginal role in society.

After Medellín, Alessio attended poetry festivals in Costa Rica, El Salvador, Nicaragua, Venezuela, Argentina, Mexico, and once more in Colombia. Back in Rome, he founded the online literary review *Fili d'aquilone*, which—availing itself of a professional editorial team of international breadth—would go on to host contemporary poetry from Québec, Colombia, Slovenia, Brazil, Portugal, Mexico, Spain, as well as unpublished work by a younger generation of Italian poets. In 2011 he founded Edizioni Fili d'Aquilone, an independent press dedicated to presenting to the Italian public international poets in their original language alongside the Italian translation. Our collaboration and friendship began in that context, when my translation of Brazilian poet Narlan Matos was published in Alessio's press (2016). Two more projects followed, which introduced to the Italian reader the work of American poet Christopher Merrill (2017), and Chilean writer Carmen Berenguer (2021). Meanwhile, I had become interested in translating Alessio's own poetry, whose stark brevity, I thought, could transfer well to the English language. A first translation of three of his poems came out in *Gradiva: An International Journal of Italian Poetry* in 2018.

Miniature Cities is the first book-length English translation of Alessio's work, an anthology of his entire oeuvre up to 2021 (13 poetry collections) that—for the most part—reflects the Italian anthology *Città in miniatura* (2021).

For reasons of space, I will not dwell on each of the individual collections herein represented, but rather limit myself to pointing out a few thematic traits that remain consistent throughout his oeuvre. One motif that dominates these texts is the sense of a struggle to maintain a precarious balance in a world teetering on the edge of chaos. A deceptively simple diction is ruptured by sudden logical leaps that evoke the little anxieties besetting our everyday lives. The poet often pauses on the fraught silence that precedes or follows disaster, the shock of a crumbling bridge, the sudden realization of having failed your partner or your children, the ambush of a devastating identity crisis ("There was a dead man in my bed but I didn't know him", p. 33).

But the roots of trauma run deeper than our individual lives: they are one with the human condition, its traces quietly preserved in the land. As we follow the poet in his bucolic meanderings, random signs of collective, historical trauma routinely leap out at us, blindsiding us like epiphanic eruptions of a repressed truth. The "golden masks of ancient shamans" (p. 47) may stare at us from the bottom of a Colombian lake. All of a sudden there is "blood everywhere / the blood of parents who have lost a son in the war" (p. 69). A hike in the woods can lead to the ruins of a lost civilization, a buried city tangled in vines (p. 85). If we dig a hole in the ground we might well find "glass shards / dazzling fragments / of Roman mosaics" (p. 11). By the same token, the splendid majesty of the Mediterranean sea conceals the bodies of African refugees shipwrecked off the coast of Italy. "The faces swollen / with burns over the neck, legs, ribcage" (p. 75), they lie at the bottom of the sea along with their dreams of better circumstances.

The true gravitational center of Alessio's poetics, the land (his Roman land in particular) bears the marks of human endeavor and suffering, guards the memory of all things achieved and lost. But it also offers a crucial antidote to pain by providing a space of calm recollection from which we can rethink our perspective on life and perhaps come to terms with our impermanence. The actions of plowing a field, planting a tree, plunging our hands in the dirt are succor for our angst-ridden existence. But they also amount to a potent metaphor for the practice of writing. For Brandolini, poetry is, indeed, "like tilling a field, rigorously and passionately, like tending a vineyard that will end up yielding scant but precious fruit" (*On Poetry*).

The poet puts his ear to the ground and hears the beat of something greater than himself— although not necessarily more meaningful. Things decay and die, random accidents happen in nature, too: a sudden freeze may kill the blooms, a tree may become diseased and fall. Yet nature is a place he keeps returning to in times of distress, a place where his anxiety disperses into the air and the tyrannical demands of his ego wash away in the river.

And nature need not be always at hand. Writers always take their little plots of land along with them, the blank pages they fill with markings, with the same painstaking humility with which farmers turn over their fields. The tight connection between land and writing is also the driving force behind Brandolini's inexhaustible curiosity for exploring new lands, both in person and through the voices of fellow-poets who live in them. In this, he highlights the unique coincidence of singularity and universality that is the paradox of writing: a practice distilled in utter solitude that nonetheless has the power to transcend all boundaries and forge a universal bond among the people of the world. In the poet's own words:

> For me writing poems was a way to reflect more sharply, remove myself from chaos, dive into silence and calmly swim on the page, across the blank space, and fill it with markings, with words. Writing poems was a chance to go far away and walk in places filled with the echo of everybody's footfalls, and then show up in the town piazza to resume my humble work, because the poetic language transports you to other worlds, other lands. It makes you talk about yourself, but as if you were someone else. (*On Poetry*, my translation)

Giorgio Mobili
3/11/23

About the Author

An Italian poet, translator, and publisher, Alessio Brandolini (b. 1958) grew up on a farm perched on the Roman hills, often helping out his father in the field. He came of age in the Years of Lead (1970s), a period of social and political unrest in which acts of terrorism were the order of the day. Just a few days after the 1978 killing of Aldo Moro, he enlisted in the Carabinieri. While in the service, Alessio managed to attend university, from which he graduated *cum laude* in Modern Italian Letters. Throughout it all, he never stopped reading, studying, and writing poetry. His verse evinces the rough serenity of country life and the horror of quotidian violence as a never fully resolved dialectics. A land that bears the marks of war, genocide, and ruined civilizations is simultaneously a hallowed space of recollection to which the poet can return to soothe the pain of existence. In Alessio's poetry, the oft-depicted actions of plowing a field, planting a tree, or digging in the dirt amount to a potent metaphor for the practice of writing. This inextricable bond between land and writing has also fueled Brandolini's lifelong passion for exploring new countries and disseminating their poetic voices through his literary press.

About the Translator

Born and raised in Milan, Italy, Giorgio Mobili — a poet, translator and teacher — has been living in the US for the last twenty-five years. He is married to a Chilean woman, which has made him an enthusiastic denizen of the Spanish-speaking world. His own creative writing (in Italian, English and Spanish) has been an attempt to reconcile this odd triangulation. In the absence of a ship designed for space and time travel, he has found that poetry is the next best thing: a synchronous dreamscape where here and there, past and now, Self and Other interact and transform into ever-new formations down the sunken boulevards of the unconscious mind. Like the walls of an anonymous hotel room, the lines of a poem stake out a magical territory of memory and longing in which what has vanished is, perhaps, never really lost.

Fomite

Writing a review on social media sites for readers will help the progress of independent publishing. To submit a review, go to the book page on any of the sites and follow the links for reviews. Books from independent presses rely on reader-to-reader communications.

More poetry from Fomite...

Fomite

For more information or to order any of our books, visit **fomitepress.com**